The Honeymoon Wil

The
Honeymoon Wilderness

Pier Giorgio Di Cicco

The **Mansfield** Press

National Library of Canada Cataloguing in Publication

Di Cicco, Pier Giorgio, 1949-
      The honeymoon wilderness / Pier Giorgio Di Cicco.

Poems.
ISBN 1-894469-09-7

      I. Title.

PS8557.I248H65 2002   C811'.54   C2002-903905-3
PR9199.3.D497H65 2002

      Cover Design by Gabriel Caira
      Text Design by Tim Hanna
      Cover photo by Magma Photo
      Author photo courtesy of Glen McGuire

The publication of The Honeymoon Wilderness has been generously
supported by The Canada Council for the Arts and
the Ontario Arts Council.

Mansfield Press Inc.
25 Mansfield Avenue
Toronto, Ontario, Canada
M6J 2A9
Publisher Denis De Klerck
www.mansfieldpress.net
Printed in Canada

When these poems are prayers,
they are for Father Damasus Trapp O.S.A.
This book is for Angela

Table of Contents

Preamble

Marrying God

Nights in the Country

The Simple Breeze in the Willow

Preamble

The Priest

I am not really there.
that is what tires me. invisibility.
it is exhausting. persona cristi.
it is not being there. leaving your body at home.
looking forward to it.
it is being whoever they think, the clothes they put
on you, their love, their hate, their father;
whoever they need; it is the ultimate acting,
with Christ moving your lips.

in one sense it should be tireless,
but it is like being in the air too long;
you could almost want to move through
household furniture and have supper
but not belonging has taken you to an abstract,
you are perfect for it.
when you learned to love something in everyone,
you were done for; a lease for
Christ. and you thought you were
going to the party as yourself.

one day you almost miss the man you were,
the body at the house.
what would you say to him?
rise, own yourself, forget what you know?
what is the kiss that wakes him?
what kind of stories does he like to hear?
what do you say to an exhumed ghost?
he gave his life for you that you might be
invisible, like this;

butterfly, the colour of everyone's
heart, what do you want of the corpse
you escaped?

Fraters

They were my brothers,
Father Alexius, Father Reinhardt, Placidus,
Grigoire, Cyril, Grazia, names to conjure
with, each a universe of prayer,
full of stories and miscommunication:
"the Shah of Iran is in California this month"
"where in China?". They heard nothing, but footsteps
and silences; oh some were just mean, and they
outlasted all the rest, God deciding to give them
more and more chances.

And I thought they were brilliant, and then
only human, and then distilledly so — whatever they
might have been, they were reduced to a single
stature, a statement of light or dark —
like all of us; only, they were called to figure that out
in small spaces and fixed timetables, by bells and cleanup,
by prayer and song. None of these things make anyone holy,
but deprivation of things makes for looking hard at God;
so it is that Anthony, like a bird, would bring twigs and
coloured glass back to his cell. When the monks changed rooms
they found a warehouse of the forsaken in there,
discarded things, from pilgrims and plain garbage.
It didn't make them lesser men; they knew they had
nothing to speak of and would ogle at the millionaires
on t.v., but they knew their lot.
I remember buying a radio in novitiate, and the lands it
brought me to were exotic, enough to make the world
seem much in a little.
Appreciation, then, the first big step towards gratitude.
So little had, you wound up thanking for breath, and moon,
and stars.
We'd sit together in the common room, reading papers and
telling stories of weird confessionals in the Bronx,

and the pranks in olden seminaries, of how Brother Matthew
lost his arm in the combine and bled to death before he was missed
at breakfast. None of these stories were told with grief
or more than jovial laughter, because there was no reason to resent
or mourn. God came with his pillow and took them one by one
to rest. We'd park them in the chapel, and go and pay a nightly visit,
just to say goodbye as if we'd dropped them at a junction and
would meet them again further down the line.

All gone. I am alone, as if they were calling to me, and I remember
their faith when nights become too horrible. I remember their
unmoving faces and eyes of transparency and light.

Even now I glamourize them, until I meet the children of the dark
and am surprised.
My brothers would have kept them still, like stones in the middle
of churning rapids; my brothers were moored
by as simple a thing as fifty years of bleeding and living together
and giving up illusion.
They were good boys, stodgy and
and humourless, and able to giggle. They were everything,
plainly human with no recourse to be more
than who they were.

The company of such men makes me
nostalgic. They were useless to everything,
but God.

Old Bridegrooms

Old bridegrooms becoming famous
in each other's eyes. Quandaries going
to sleep behind their eyelids. The way they lift
leaves as if to share, their hands full
of improbable zest.
An old bridegroom with every automobile, that's
what I say, with every umbrella, or singing
your children to sleep, annoying yard animals
with folkloric voices,
trying every imaginable posture against trees,
amusing each angle, defying your
photo albums with a flair and reminiscence.
Old implacable bridegrooms to be desired,
longing in the avatars of birch.
Give me an old bridegroom, resting on my back
in formal dress as I float along, accosting
the shore with surface songs.
I am done for, complete, certain at last,
searching from inlet to bay, joyous.
Away from that bitch, that bride of the world.
My dear old bridegrooms,
carnivores of time,
let us rendevous.
I know nothing about happiness, I will say to you.
I have run out of emotions.
Will you have me now?
Your eyes, like chestnuts of light, crack like smiles
as you step forward, archangels
between now and then.

That First Year

i wrote poems mainly that first year,
picking garbage, doing dishes, humbling
myself among men who doubted me for having gotten
the world's publicity; what did i want with them, anyway?
but after a year they saw my touch and needed an arm
around them; men without women can use an italian
now and again to laugh christ off the cross and make him dance;
make the devil look a bit foolish.
it was my mission, cheering them after i saw that they had not
god in every blessed fork and spoon, and signs weren't everywhere.
so i got down to the business of living,
of taking one to the zoo, another to a store, a coffeeshop; but
always they couldn't wait to get home; after awhile,
thrilled as they were to get out, they got
fatigued in the world, like inmates, like loonies.

i too get tired now, going downtown, the noise and ruckus of
portuguese youths blasting and cruising, the correct and
their brandies, the traffic money-making rush of decent
moms and dads in their illusion of house
and car, and literature taking itself seriously and anyone
taking something serious to get away from pointlessness —

i want to go back, like a loonie. not made for this.
i want to stack chairs with grigoire in
the church and go to sleep and stare at the blank
wall of the chapel and see christ's face. i want to sing
like st. john rieti who became a saint just for singing
to birds. . .

i want to see everything as a sign: something dropped, a cloud going the
wrong way; and not in a town where there
are signs everywhere, and no signs.

stillness is what i crave, like those loonies, who did nothing
but look for signs 'cause everything is a sign when you do
little.
i want grigoire's bees, anthony's galoshes galumphing
past my cell window, the scrape of chairs at breakfast
and walking down corridors with space between each
other in case the saints wanted to get through.

silly things. i want to go home.
i wait for everything but god
now; like all the others i make use of
his creation and forget —
to wait for him. . . just wait for him,
worry that he'll take me, just to get attention;
that's what the world is, a sleep-waiting;
once i was awake and nothing-doing
and when he asked me to get us a coffee, i would —
otherwise we would just sit together, god and i
with eyes that penetrated.

behind trees and things, i feel that world that's ours,
and loonie brothers playing hide-and-seek with
butterflies;
my madmen, my crazies; like you
i can't be away for far too long; wherever you are, waiting,
in death or hayfields,
call me "in-free" before dusk.

Fr. Eugene

he never did shut up, big talker
and small ego, hands sweaty after 30 years of
serving the germans or saying mass with them,
which is the same; worried to death by his shadow, and false
report and rumour, a holy loving man who loved mary, the
rosary and couldn't do anything about the
liberals dismantling his statues; talked enough about it,
but didn't do anything;
you might call it weak toilet training;
knew richard the 3rd by heart, at least three soliloquys.
when i got there, green and moony-eyed from
praying at the statues on st. clair, i took him
seriously; he said i would do this and that, and spoke of god's
will, talked of anything; neurosis — i thought you couldn't
be holy and be neurotic.

years later, i love him, his betrayals and weak ego,
inability to stand up for this and that —

but what fascinates me is that i bought everything he said
that first year, i bought anything,
not thinking monasteries were mostly
places where the helpless sought refuge when young
and slugged it out for 60 years. i thought they chose to
go there, while of course god calls in different ways —
anthony's mom beat him until his brain dislodged and the
nuns saved him and put him into a monastery; there he is
still believing in flying saucers, but he's a saint —
so are they all, these madmen.
what fascinates me, always, is that i sat with
their lunacy for years and saw god's guiding
touch in all they said and did before i knew they were
crazy; and that holied me. when you can see the
angelic in the imbecilic you're close to god.

i kinda regret my cynicism now; mind you i did
nothing the world might think productive for 4 years — cleaned flies
in alex's room, did floors, did windows, listened interminably
to loneliness i mistook for solitude; but
what you do for love comes back
to roost — that crazy coloured
bird on your shoulder or a twinkle in
your eye as you read aloud with a child's heart
or speak with the weight of 40 men, their
torture between walls and crucifixes.

i am happy i was with them;
and honey-bees and lakes and leaves falling;
there was nothing more intelligent than sitting
with the foolish, of one kind or another.

Being

"it's your choice".

i never cared to choose except to
please somebody. a sin today.
that's the way we were, altruistic.
but now it's fashionable to choose for yourself.

i am surrounded today by choices;
a beautiful day, relaxed autumn, rugs to clean
or not, time to go or not to go.
one of those moments when god has no
imperatives, and what you've accomplished

glows in the corner. what to do? choices,
and the room caves in cause there's no one
to do things for and what you do for anyone
is arbitrary in time. they'll remember you
over a coffee, a book, for as long as they
can before memory seeps into the ground
like yesterday's moisture.

someone rang the doorbell all morning while
i slept. what did they want? it must have been
so gosh-darned important, whatever it was.
everything is so damned important for awhile
and to you, 'cause they care, their choices are
everything, to anybody, anytime.

today i would choose, as i always have, to
do something extravagantly different, like tell
the world that nothing matters, but i
would do it for the world, let's face it, to
change it, while it forgets me.

and as for those who choose to make
themselves happy — call it that. i call
it christ, giving something and disappearing
behind a rock.

Deep Consonant Wife

Deep, consonant wife, strapped to my
early years, whom I will always marry; beautiful
woman in the torso of a five-year-old, plummet me through
the furniture, stupid furniture; reorient
its nature, make prayers of it for my hot mouth.
"Hot mouth!" There is a conquistador in the leaves,
you know? I have seen whole armadas of affection
in a Georgia wood, under the loon's call; a kitten
on a stump of a tree looking like a snake in the
moonlight, and when I got closer its hot little
mouth was whiskered with weather and cricket sounds
and an aftertaste of moonlight. Just so, wife!

You, before the voyage, after which everything
else was after-wife, was after-life, was me with
a hologram of myself ahead of me. Blue sheaf of
a patch of sky, woman with a necklace of my chromosomes,
be here, wife with a thousand and one poems coming to you,
make me; every morning a virgin in your hands
— that's what I am, behind
the suit of hours, years; come out from behind the
furniture, my warehouses of thought, and plunge your
white palms into me. Cup my face like a sun among clouds
and make the widowing earth green with envy.
Break me among my stupidities,
among my men,
my projections,
give me that twig, out there, outside my window.
Let us look at it for the first time, again,
like a planned marriage among the stars in the stone.

Some Self-Reflection

a bit of a codger.
an american codger.
not just playful, a little "furbo".

i learned from bro. anthony
to act a little crazy and they'd leave you
alone.

then there's the survivor
from my father's camps and
ambushing the rival gangs from
the dundalk woods.

growing up smelling danger, separating
it from the scent of hyacinths.

then there's the plain old sincere one
who can't hide from god;

who won't confuse charity with his own need,
who puts christ in front of him
when his own heart is salivating.

don't confuse the both of them.
the songster from tuscany,
the sleeper with one eye open,
the feminist nightmare,

the one who knows where this poem is going
but is open to the turn
in the neck of the woods.

a simple guy,
with a knowledge of human nature,

owing to nothing but death,
a plain birdsong,
and the resurrection of his mother,

the world.

Marrying God

Marrying God

I

my god blesses forks and spoons,
and bad sex and bad livers and pontiac chrome,
chickens and silence. he sifts crowds of busy people
through his hands like sand and wakes me with
new scripts. he doesn't give a hoot for health,
he owns everything in the junk shop and says, here
take it, walk out with it.
my god vomits convention and spells evil like
expectation, is soft. he has my mother's eyes
without her edicts. his tragedy is holiness in
special places. he blesses pots and pans in dime stores.
he visits.

•

yes, and that too.
he says you made a mistake, the bigger,
the better. hello you, hello god beginning to
appear. god who discards vestments and vessels,
god made badly of new age crystals and environmental
texts, you who don't know what to do with feminists,
bishops and bad popcorn.
god who blesses lonely canes and tadpoles on the
wash of the chesapeake, god who blesses serbians and
greeks and bad food, god who doesn't know how to
transcend cultural barriers and says enjoy what you
got and invent more things to bless.

god who opened my eyes in a field, in a wood,
on a day when walt whitman came to me and trains
and the declaration of independence written in my
heart like the will to live; god who doesn't climb
into mausoleum crypts with hysterical calabrians,
who reads bad poetry and calls it bad.

god as hungry as i am, as you are, for indian chutney and
healing the sick. he says i made a mistake listening
for him in the house of fear, the bad angels of
socialists and such. come thou to the church of
thistle and bramble, build me a treehouse of things you like
away from mother and the shouts of the diseased,
the ones who have splayed imagination like a horse's
carcass on the streets where you live.

●

and he loves me. my stupid guilt
i hate, he permits it, he has surfing to do,
he runs ahead to the beach, come or don't come,
that's free will; romp or don't, build your cathedral
of "don't", hurt everyone inside yourself; the coney
island goes on, the play, the shrieks of joy; stay home.
my god comes home, with nothing to say to my
brooding. he is savvy, he loves me but won't
eat my bad bread.

●

i don't know what he does with compasson.
i think if you don't surf, or can't swim, he may give you
lessons; the point is he gives you something you can do.
and that's kindness. he sees your misery
and opens the windows, lets some clean air in, heals
your rheumatism, maybe a phone call from a friend or a shard
of hope. i suspect he forgives bad habits on their way
to something good, i suspect he locks murderers up with
stupid people who can't be murdered. i suspect he is
very serious about your needs crushing a flower or a laugh.
i suspect my despair is his darkest moment and i curse him for
my unwillingness to climb out. i suspect he has locked me in my room
and then find he has left a key under the sheets.
i do not know the name of that game. i may be locking myself in.
it's maybe satanic. it's maybe lack of imagination that

kills hope, and that's done by listening to the unimaginative:
relatives, employers, school systems and t.v. watchers;
prudes too have their way, they are pedagogues, the politically correct
and mothers who think their children are always in danger
at any given moment;
fear is what prudes are about; they make by-laws and privatize
beaches.

•

god is pulling the blinds down, he is shutting off the day —
these gates called morning and sunset. funny that he sets up
parameters to his fun-lovingness; anything can take place,
a world of inventions and marvel, but you can't skeet shoot
at night. funny god. you can climb into another person's soul
in a moment of love any time, but you need a flashlight in the woods.
just once i wish he would light up midnight with something
other than conversation. nature; they call it the nature of
things, but why he doesn't muck with it is beyond me. he'll
suspend the tempest so the rescuers can reach the survivors, but
why not dispense with the tempest altogether?
bad weather, good weather, day and night, everything has a purpose,
but why the structure? it's beyond me.
why not have morning come at three in the afternoon?
things are the way they are. and what does that say about
god, about this dancer, this gardener, this lover?
he loves some formalism; but has poets stay up
until others go to work. funny guy.
no wonder the ancients thought there were two gods, or three,
no wonder they worshipped nature and particles,
and chance, those mini-gods with different by-laws.
the mega-paradigm of love weaves through the fabric of all,
but what is the point of not being able to walk through walls?
there's a certain lack of economy in you, god.
what is the point of clocks if time stands still
when you look into a lover's eyes?
my god, you worry me, your structuralism, and you want me
to be a deconstructivist! if digital sequence is the fall from the

garden, why seek wholeness from your children?
if dark is the absence of light why give us venetian blinds?
to make bad poetry? and there you are again pulling the blinds down on
another day. there you are again, beyond me.

•

he doesn't say much.
doesn't keep to himself really, goes out a lot,
talks in smiles mostly, your smiles.
ever ask him if he loves you? the smile on your
face is what he says, the smile of another, the
phone call at the right moment, the nice surprise,
the good things, countless; but
he doesn't say much, really; he leaves naming to adam
and poets and lovers; he says the occasional thing to joan of arc
and moses — private revelation for the most part.
but ask him why you're happy or not and what happened to uncle
willie, he'll answer with a turn
of cloud, a ripple on a pond.
just doesn't like words; odd, for the "word made flesh" — for
logos — strange — doesn't even like words for himself —
the nameless, unnameable — doesn't like being pinned
down, but loves being found, my lonely orphan god,
so emotionless and so passionate,
so eager for the unmute and so mute, so
happy with poems and songs and always without an escort,
with his angels and seraphs trafficking like grand central
station, sending messages of love everywhere, everywhere,
yet speechless to the drama of my heart.
never says much and gets my attention so often.
this god of mine whom i am deaf to in my folly.
for whom i need a language to love.

•

he sends me her, he sends me him, he sends me
beauty in forms i understand an angel woman,
an angel-man; he sends me incarnations
to learn from, to hymn, to make a hymn; he sends me
those who must wind up in heaven, they were so lovely.

he sends flowers, nightlights, he sends memories and
dreams relived. he sends schopenhauer, don't ask me why,
and louts and letters that arrive late.
he sends satellite t.v. that flashes no signal in a storm.
he sends an apprehension, a premonition, he sends a promise
that turns like a bitter rind in my mouth, he sends tomorrow
in a dream of death.

he appears as sunset and canyon, as ruby lips and caress,
he appears as time and has none.
he sings in words from my mouth, those serenades
that waft around his head like fireflies in the musky fields.
he sings in my mouth, like a heart outside of me,
hoping i will appear as he, the one incarnation that marries me,
and then we will understand each other.
he sends me to myself until i answer,
a beauty untrammelled, and recognized in each and every
love.

II

she says god is a cold experience —
the touch of him;
bill says time is there because of things
invented by god; another says you are fire.
many ideas of you.
i don't remember anything about you,
except you grabbed my throat,
and brought tears to my eyes when i heard
a robin sing. brother vincent used to hear music when
you wanted him.
i don't know where you go when the child is buried,
or if you hold my mother's hand in the soil.
i don't know where you are when the fireman
finds his son in the smouldering house.
i know you are happy to see me on the avenue,
strutting my stuff. i know you hate to eavesdrop.
i sift ideas of you for others.
i am the prospector. i see the nugget, the
abandoned mine. i have an idea what claims are useless —
oh let us sit down where you have nothing to say.
be cold, be hot, i know you, fed up with attention and
jealous too; mercy is the only name you have. the rest
is our business.
but let us sit awhile like two bounty
hunters on a hunt for beauty, yours in mine and mine in
you. let us rest the night. a good coffee, and rest the night.
painting the stars and whippoorwill with a wave of your hand
that tucks me in, your little cowboy, and the ideas of you
so far away like lone coyotes doing their music,
so irrelevent, like everything else, and useful.

•

you give me breath, you give me sun,
you clear the conduits of brains
to bring me scents, memories. you remind
us of picnics together; you fill time with
an hour of life lusting, you send hope and
coupled birds and mock me with an unending.
you send another day with no projects,
you go from room to room, arranging knick-knacks
and clocks. you leave letters like an idea
here and there. you say go to sleep.
your undemandingness amazes. do nothing,
something. i weave you into the fabric of all,
and it is enough for you.
i marvel at the faucet's drip while your other hand
soothes burned skin on the far side of the
planet. companion to everything, omniflowering
one, whose eyes are for me alone, alone for everyone,
how do you come without bells and knocks;
how do you visit, the heart so errant?
where do you run to, luck in your wake, for all of us;
grace for a crown — how do you plank the sunset on
silos, and kiss the widow, and bank on me?
you bring me scents, and now, you bring me sleep,
and no trouble, respite of you, your passion, for the
wake to the awful emotionality you are.
my tempest, god.

•

your surprises are a bit much;
the bad news on the phone after a good day,
it's like you don't want to be typed a good guy,
like you want to keep me on my toes.
i've grown used to your surprises, the rap on the head
after the banana with whipped cream on it.
it's getting so it spoils your gifts,
as if i didn't appreciate your winning smile
without your mandarin hurts.

if i did everything well, would that do it?
i had the clammy feel of crucifixion once;
i climbed down, baffled.
you want me between too much fun
and too much weeping, and you miss the rendezvous.
almost, you want me to ignore you
and get on living,
and yet you make me want you;
i want to know you but not have you.
because you blow hot and cold where the air is thin.

•

what do you make of my father walking
down lennox street in baltimore looking for
italian magazines or of his phonograph albums —
mantovani in the basement, his new movie camera,
the way he tied his tie? what do you think?
did he buy mantovani because he was italian,
and. . . say! what was the point of shipping him
overseas to southern accents, a man fumbling an
accordion, looking for ristorantes instead of
corvettes and things; what is the point, forty years
later, of my playing his albums for him and polishing his
movie camera etc.? at least i got a priest's collar instead of
a tie. saved me some trouble.
forget the pathos. i have to know. . . are you walking
him where he doesn't need translation, are you showing him
the best shops, are you getting him a spot on the lawrence welk
show where he can tan with his accordion on santa monica
beach? he'd like that, santa monica sounding italian and all.

do you take care of your own?
do you fill in those gaps that would have made life
liveable — a handy espresso bar, the sound of
friendly people having a coffee, a hello in the language of
your birth? or maybe you take him in a corvette down the
highways of nevada and show him what his son learned to
like. what do you do with those who pined away?
i know. you give me his things and more, you say enjoy them
for the dead, forget their hunger.
i say, look after them. leave me in peace;
let me catch a glimpse of both of you behind some trees
sharing a joke with a good glass of wine; let me see you
laughing out of the corner of my eye as i bumble
towards my bank, or love, or ruination.
give me that peace and give my regards to the
loved, the ones with the hole plugged where the
heart leaked out for love of you.

●

when he died, i cursed the aspersion of holy water
on his coffin by a strange man with a collar on.
i looked at the ground and said,
what is my father doing there?
i didn't understand resurrection or the blessing that
passes even through hypocrisy. the priest that day
who blessed a simple man who never went to church
died of his wifeless god and trailed pounds of grief
for the unknown he ushered groundwards. he too understood
nothing, like my father — just walking the planet in good
faith, knowing that doing good was the next best stop
to hell on earth; never mind understanding god.

i bless them both,
and cactus and lively things that almost die,
flowers and children; i cast holy water on the
heads that bloom towards their
creator, but dumb with the cataract of
living, dumb with hypocrisies, and tired of
perfection that keeps them from putting down a blanket
and sleeping in the noonday sun.

when my father died i said — what are you doing in the
cold ground, what kind of god puts you on the
bottom side of the house you paid for and lived in?
forty years later i sprinkle holy water on my mother's
grave and know she is not there.
seeing is not believing, then? so long to teach your
son metaphysics? to understand
resurrection and my own damned faults?

to the fourteen year old boy at my father's
funeral i say, dry your tears, and take
nothing seriously. no one is ever qualified
to bless the dead, but everyone and you.
and don't do it with tears. do it casually,
the way god gives birth and eternity.

III

you giveth and you taketh.
frankly you can keepeth for all i care.
what am i, a see-saw?
you're worse than fickle, you change your
mind every few seconds.
you give a beauty and you lose it for me.
am i undeserving? then cut the
dreams from my brain, the ideal this and that.
but where would you store them
but in the nutshell of some patsy called humankind.
not armadillos, not anything could scurry so well between
double binds as a lover in the heyday of his nightmare.
my mother's happy time, everybody's special time,
before the goths of chance
pillage the heart.
she also said, take it as it comes, when she was out of faith.
and i beseiged her for lacking faith.
it was you who held back, you who give enough to finish
cathedrals and pietas before a smack of
pestilence or plague.

it's no wonder an army of atheists
and feminists remove your granite steps
and fashion you to likeness. is illusion more a sin
than missing church? is that why you forgive the
ignorant, because they're on track, hearing that faint
primordial croak you gave, saying "forget me"?

some of us heard badly, heard "love me",
some heard the ancestral cry of want.
i want you to be around, dispensing and not
taking back your gifts; if it pleases you
i'll forget you. if you want remembering
kiss me when i wake, without metaphor;

no sunny day, no songs, just your lips on my forehead
like an anointing; the oil, the sweat of labour
to be near you.

•

"smoking can kill you" — funny the signs you put on
packages, the stuff you print by way of your
droogies; as if i hadn't died of love, of death of
others, of beatings, of remembered passion.
what warnings did we have of the things that really did us in?
or do we think that if we live the good life we'll
die predictably? no, not like that, not you —
lover of surprises.
as if looking both ways to keep from being run down
were helpful. it helps. . . everything helps.
but here's that god who appears with doves and rabbits up his
sleeve; applause is due, between the wailing and bloodletting,
applause is due, is owing; here it is. . .
"i love you.
you are the true warlock".
but if it were my wand i would have
filled the doomed embrace of lovers with an
endless spring.

•

do you remember
the men marching to chapel,
brother anthony's birds, the weep and wail
of novices clambering for the holy?
were you in the marble steps,
in the hand of st. joseph in the half-dark,
in the snowy pines and the raphaelite clouds?

were you in the hands of father alex fumbling for his rosary
and the crippled hands of laudislaus at the organ?
were you in basil's voice or anthony's hand on the light-

switch of the corridor;
were you happy at lauds and salve regina,
were you casting dice with the statues in the attic?
were you in the dust in the cloister library?
were you keeping memories for all of us

were you there at all?

•

nothing much matters to you.
not guilt, not good times, not anything.
i know this. this too is vanity.
it passes. . . the next good thing, the glory, laughter;
all that's left is your stone silence, eternality.
i tell them what they'll get to heaven by is
love, its lightness, wings —
that rancor makes the trip impossible.
but i don't know; i help them live good
lives by what you give to me.
it's hard. i wake to my sermonizing and
suddenly you want to play — when my body is
bulletted with pain and the chemo is bombing
them out in the front pew and the widow
asks me why. sometimes i am so eloquent, i
want to run out amidst the cattle on the hill
and make palettes of the evening sun.
i think poetry is what i bring them.
"art gives hope", neruda said.
it seems i'm never out of art as you throw another
log on the fire of me, another thing, your use of me.
i know there's only prayer.
and that's why you clam up.
there's nothing to say, really. vanity is
fuss over the obvious.
you are the woodsman carving love,
we are the children with fool questions —
what are you making, old man? how old are you?

i don't know how i got to talking about you.
i went to a monastery to pray. they
wouldn't shut up there either.
i would have taught stone silence to the world
like a lilac breeding from stone;
and here i am, sermonizing.

you see, so much matters to them.
what matters to me
is my irreparable mouth.
and why you need it.

IV

they're singing
"let's build a stairway to the stars" on the radio;
i like that.
today i don't know if i have
any feelings. somedays i think i repress them,
other days, i weep in the shower, other days
blood runs from my arms, thinking of
mortality. i am soothed by
"twenties" love songs all week long and the ocean of love
between lovers that are no more.
i am moved by jimmy stewart and
donna reed under a moon; i am moved by other peoples'
feelings, not my own; i am stunned with burying people,
baptizing them, being grabbed at.

once, i fell asleep
to visions of children playing.
i'd like to sleep like that again. . .
but really, i have no feelings.
i have everybody's feelings.
that's the problem.
how do you deal with your feelings.
do you still have them? are you tired?

have you left me alone with
tiredness, to bring me close to you?
you make me see through everything,
until i'm passionless. i don't want
that. i want to stay in your creation.
you leave me with
twenties songs and then, tomorrow with less.
we go through everything, boxes and boxes
until there's only sunlight coming
through an attic window.

•

where are you when we need you?
you who have lost my faith.
if sin corrodes faith, hope and charity, i've sinned;
it's where saro committed suicide; yet
you give faith to the atheistic and the schoolgirl, you guide
them along the abyss of incomprehension
as you did me, before i could spell sacrament.
i might almost do it on my own.
we call you "providence" when we're not
in control. i have been out of control.
and it wasn't fight i ran out of, but beauty —
the wonder, that such and such exists in spite of me;
for some the fighting ends with a poem
or a beautiful woman,
and something dialogues besides fear;
volition takes a break and
finds a partner.

when did you unpartner me?
or is it just my thirst for you
that disinherits me?

•

your poetry is prayer —
everyone joining in and
speaking the poem with you.
all words boil down to basics:
love me, forgive me,
need me, thank you. everything else
is a warming up. everyone everywhere craving
the simple, getting dressed for it
and making noise.
but you, you want few words for what it takes
to get us swimming; you let us spell fear, hate, worry,
and you send angels to shove us in.
with me it takes near-death

to smell a flower, to see rain clouds as sun cover,
to see love in the paranoid.

to consecrate the world to the
celestial is what i want, in one instant — the dance
that is almost flight, the hello kiss that is
bequeathment, the eulogy woven in the membrane
of petals, given as a bouquet to those i love.

to never leave you out. that is my dream, to open
someone's hand to show you there. to give us back,
your gifts.

●

he fell into my arms and said
"sometimes god takes what we love most. he knows best".
i agree.
so i made up something as i buried his grandchildren.

i said, "god wants us to love him unconditionally";
to get too tired to be angry; to love him
the way my friend zorab goes into the niagara gorge
to look for messages in bottles. he hates god, but finds hope.
you get thankful for anything
he doesn't take: breath, sight,
memory, until they're taken. then you're thankful
for death.
such gratitude, taking everything for
granted, your ski-doos, your anger, sorrow;
even fear; you fork
over every feeling to him.

today i am thankful for anything,
even the cold glance of
those who do not love me. it's an experience.

my novice master used to say he couldn't be
hurt anymore. me? i collect every sight and sound i'll
miss in my final moment.

today i buried four children. i don't know what the weeping
was about; i held the
grandfather's head to my own, like a
horrified brother faced with an
unconditional god. it was like holding my own head.
his brain, his love, his faith, my own — and
doing what we do best — living in spite of him.
until he opens the screen door and says, come in;
the day of streets and leaves is over.
lay your head to rest, and put away
the likeness of the day.

V

being married to you is not much different
from being married to a woman, really.
you have your good days and your bad days.
you're not there in the flesh, that's all, unless
i'm an artist and i see you in flowers
and spoons falling.
you nag too, talk too much or too little, tell
me the house is untidy. you let me go out
to show me i got it good at home. you let me
see you in everyone and their eyes only
reflect you, oh spirited wife, for whom i am too carnal,
for whom i grow to bridehood.
shall we walk around the house invisible one day
or will i see you as you are, visible in everything,
not a pot, not a corner without you?
i could then take joy in raising glasses to my friends,
and my life, and be complete.
that's what holiness is. . . completeness. it's nothing to do
with love or being loved as i had said.

"what you are looking for is what is looking", st. francis said.
why are your eyes opaque to me?
is it my cataracts? is it my soul? here, i'll clean it.
is it my yearning that must be perfect before you
appear out of thin air? what do you want to hear?
why this silence that deafens me into your arms?

be with me when i go to the store.
beat me mercifully with aches and pains.
don't flirt with me in public.
these words are a wounded letter
take them for what they are.

•

i remember the seminarian with a lisp practising his homily and
saying the wise men brought gifts of frankincense and
mirth; everyone laughed,
then got serious.
but i think if i were a wise man i would have
tickled you in the manger as i would any baby;
maybe i don't understand the glow
of cosmicness around your baby's heart in me,
maybe the sacred shouts for dead silence,
maybe the dance is what one does before that.
maybe one dances and falls into stone still adoration,
and dances again; maybe it's both you want,
and this frenzied poem is dervish to
my wonderment.

do you want me to be quiet?
i'll pray in monkish silence
or walk among
the pilgrims as i did,
dressed in long robes,
holding babies

and tickling them for love of
you the way the angels did at christmas and in
paintings; well they don't tickle you exactly
but they amuse you from a reverent
distance don't they?

is this the gift before you send me packing
to the land i came from? i am not so wise.
my life is changed by seeing in the crib
the eyes of a child; they are my own, so
gracious and so pained
with the cross and laughter mixed.
and my hands move erratically
as those of a baby, wanting to make
something of the air — a poem,

a face, an incarnate job —
so down to earth,
the celestial in us.

•

bill calls, wants to go horseback riding;
the trails are waiting, he says; there you are,
that's what you say — never mind the dance and
silence, go riding. you fool me every time. i
peg your voice and you say go surfing, horseback
riding, go to arcturus; how can i deny you?
though i can't do any of those things very well;
i fear water, i have hemorrhoids and i fly
real bad to starlight. still, you laugh, you're
tickling me, not i you.
that's the god i love, there you are, shining
broadly like the landscape's smile, saying
take everything seriously but life;
leave that to me.

•

here i am writing madly, as prayer,
or final will, as if i were wildly packing
to join my dead brothers, as if a
line here or there
might expiate the botch i made of
thinking ill of others, damaging myself.
expiation and thrill, that's me,
that's the pole i balance, walking on a highwire
while the oohs and ahhs below
both scare and goad me.
when shall i have peace? when i walk
to the other end of the wire? when i get there
do i bow, have an espresso hoisted up and point to the
hole above in the tent where your
smile pokes through, saying "well done"?

or are you just another spectator,
surprised to see me make it through,
to see your children walk
for the first time?

there are so many possibilities, they fall
to silence at last; the bones don't crush,
there's a net below; but sometimes the
wondrous is exhausting or dumbfounding.
when there's so much you allow, i'm humbled
into sleep, a meditation.

VI

the faucet drips. it mocks me.
better if it were the words of someone.
the fleshed out memory of lovers, poignant
beauties under starlight and lamplight.
i don't care for my body anymore.
nothing hurts like the missing ones in you.
the ones he primed you with, you still want.
primed you for him. you look at your knuckles,
the changing geography of skin, and you are
getting dressed for him as the body gets shucked
until you are just heart, beating in an open field
for him to take you; what was the flesh about, the
caressing, the tenderness trained on cheeks and
flowing hair, dad's bristly beard, my mother's
sagging but plenteous forearm; what was the walk
on leaf-filled streets for, hand in hand, past this
lump in my throat for all the nostalgia
of share with the human creature, beatified
by care and cradling?
trained, trained for what? why the flesh
when you want it erased into your smile? `
why not have come down from a cloud before that
father? what was it for, the dance, the song
remembered, the anniversary of eyes;
divinity is stones mounted like stairs, but made of
heartbreaks, joys? would i not have come to you
without the bramble of kiss and stroke?
would i have desired your contours when you don't
have them? what is the shape of your face, god?
let me feel it, let me touch it like a blind man
whose ears are filled with music,
earthly songs, of angels made of flesh and bone.
why the narrative of touch when you won't shape
your face for me, past these hungry and stupid fingers?

•

here i am alone with you
again on a friday afternoon
with the sun going down being drawn down
whatever you are doing with it with your
puppetry, your masterful whatever;
what have you done to my heart, pulled
the shutters on that too and made it race
to a loved one? today you keep it still, relatively
still as if you rested between the beats;
a moment of conversation within the heartbeats,
one word between every beat maybe, saying,
after enough of them, "i love you, i love you;
be not weary, let the world pass"; the sunset like
a closing door i could almost pass through
if i hurry, in time.
but i don't feel hurried today.
i am tired. you say rest. want nothing, need
no one, the flowers of those you love, hold them
up in your left hand, you tell me, like a flame,
like a tribute; like a sun that takes the
place of the one setting.

•

giving is such a casual, blessed thing; i have a string
of beads, of giving, i trail right down the corridor,
down the neocortical alleys, down shafts of
remembrance. do you remember all the giving?
you were there, by the side, watching the botch-up,
carousing with a glass of wine in your hand
when i did it right, and ah those exquisite moments when
i knew you were watching and the three or more of us
smelled incarnate. and how about those evenings when i told
the girl there was nothing to be afraid of in the dark
and i wasn't convinced? you left the room, to say

you're going to have strength for this, giving when i
didn't have much to give; and the heart blossomed like
a flower in the dark; i never waited till morning to bloom,
to open up my petals, did i?
they'll say that much about me; "he waited for the moment
not being right" — to break the windows open and let the birds
of celerity blast into someone's heart. like pigeons fluttering
in a bell tower when we stumble on them, expecting the halfdark
when the window blasts open, dust scatters, and whiteness like
wings in spirit cheers the lonely.
i did that for a hundred friends.

do that to me now, for me. my heart is a fearful attic;
the sun has set. let me feel your kiss between heartbeats,
in that engine i have so poorly treated with stupid scares
and cigarettes. manage me like you do sunset and those
i have strengthened. let them find sunrise without me.
but for now, scatter the pigeons, tear the musty curtains
down, scatter the dust in me; whiten in the black light of
my faith, as pathetic a thing as loneliness.
take the lump in my throat and make it a fireball —
a meteor to run with train whistles and the simple
breeze in willows.

Christmas Suite

let me do my office;
anne phones, dutifully, widowed and
depressed at 70 years plus; doesn't seem that
old at this time of my life. stuck in
a high rise in mississauga, mourning
jack's death of 15 years ago; she still sends
me mass cards for him and always asks me if i have
time to say mass for him — as if i didn't ever have
time to say mass for him, all the dead.
the first snowfall of the year. she can't see past
the mist from her 20th floor apartment.
who can?
in the midst of my befuddlement
in the twenty-first century, she reminds me
there are those no less grieved than i.
merry christmas, jesus; your eyes will
shine from some manger at some moment
in the next few weeks
and bring hope, you little poet you.
bring less snow for those for whom snow
reminds them of the painful and bring more
snow for those who toboggan, build snowmen
and are in love;
have fewer people die for a day or two,
give some a reason to get out of bed, and
for those who can't, give them a resignation,
a sweet snow blanketing, of you, your will;
and theirs, so patient.

•

last year you gave us a humdinger of a christmas;
this year a hollow one. how is it it can be
the best or worst of times?
how much love is in the heart?
how does grace fall?

does a prayer work? it seems like
a tired wand tonight.
others can get through it. me? i have
to muster up fidelity and blue notes
to say five christmas masses for those who only
come once a year to hear a message of hope.
i'm going to oil all the moving parts for that one.
oh it must be nice to hibernate, to hole up,
just mope along the avenue — but to
medley words of hope

when i don't feel them!
ah this will please the anti-catholics
and scandalize the innocent and hopeless;
i will keep this as a secret between you and i,
god; i walk through snowflakes like they were
gadflies in summer; i see christmas lights like the
lights of a trawler, from deep down in the
water, i see smiles and they don't fool me.
maybe they weren't supposed to fool me,
that's the problem — i've always tried to be
convinced by signs of happiness, smelled
inauthenticity and danced in spite of it.
but today i feel no dance, oh lord.
i feel no shopping in me. your incarnations
fail me.
i should have written you a poem last christmas.
oh yes, i did, said thank you. you heard it.
did it hurt your feelings? did your wisdom
balance it out, that joy, this badness?
or is xmas no different a time for you
than any other.
every day of your lives, you say, is a ledger
of dance or burial.
still this is a sign, is it not? a memorial,
this crib thing with stars and wise men.
make it not a time of irony, give anne her husband
back, give me an angel, give my sleeping

mother a good son, and a thousand harmonicas
for my father.
make the seasons worth something,
and this one too;
this poem is not a present to you,
but use it, if you must. . .
to exchange your gift of
grace, for a memory of christmas past,
with a tag that says "what for".

●

having said that,
am i damned in thanklessness?
no, there is a time for thanklessness.
it is your blood flowing in us,
the passionate, the christ, so take this
cup from me, if it be thy will;
and i always mean "your" will; but don't
expect understanding from the passionate;
"*passio*" means to suffer, "*compassio*" means to
suffer with, and i suffer with you, for
your thankless children. i am what you suffer
for and what suffers with you; i am the
halfway man, the fully conscious and
not quite awake,
i am omega-climber, job, the thief on the cross;
i am many personifications, without the lesson
learned. let's see, what is the lesson?
to not give a shit to stay in this world,
and suddenly to see the world freshly, no
one thing prettier than another;
and that's the catch, just once or many times
you send a prize, a joy, a person, who crowns your
giving. "don't make too much of that" you say — for
you will take it from us, so we can see the world
as democratically as you do.
but don't you see gradations? don't you love some things

more? — humility, a giving, sacrifice?
your problem is you want to see the carnal done
abstractly and the divine done with hearts of
moderate passion. i am not moderate.
i'm not your john of the cross or teresa of avila;
i am your screamer. i want gabe and so and so and angela
and all the beautiful smiles
and happy saints corralled; i am the ranchero that
gathers horses, not sheep from your pastures.
i am your demi-god, creation,
winning the purpose of creation, not sitting
for idle messages and wondering irony and ironing out
my will like stencils for your windowpane.
i am your screamer. get used to it.
i will take everyone off the cross,
and dance with them.

•

almost, i do not care. things hurt
less and less, with no less passion,
except for your seductress, beauty. the thing
i cobweb like a spider is the thing
that snags me, a walking beauty, or the
earth gussied up with morning dew.
i get attached to your masterpieces
and you make me see another, make another.
i want to rest and look, like a tourist in a
gallery, like a curious visitor at the
back of a church; just gaze at what's been done.
just rest in heaven, in the mona's eyes.
just gaze, pizzaro on the ocean coast;
not adore, just live, and make a habitat of wonder.
"you are an explorer", says a metaphoric friend.
no. i am a man foiled in creation, the angel who did
not want to come, but with a bit of goodness
in him, and half-deaf, who does your bidding, loves,
your children and hears badly new directives.

i am your child, your childless demi-god,
your passion you have not the guts to strut
yourself; i have a long hurrah awaiting me
when i get back. but i'll be humble, exhausted
at your feet when i return. i will have forgiven you; or,
rather — have forgotten all the hurt by your divine light;
wake me, father, and let the job of day be done.

●

it is a friday afternoon. the snow is darkened
and my friends are gathered in coffee shops
in town, glad that the week is done.
i sit between coyotes, stags and starlight and the
those i take care of — each readying in his
own way — the coloured ribbons, the forgetting
of the dead loved one, the slaps on the back after
the toast, the jokes, the countless inane jokes;
the tired christmases in the eyes of the 90 year
old widow. one crib, one set of eyes, to say so much
to a whole world.
and i am no different, as i am; collecting me,
as you do, with all the other prayers and preparations
and resolves.
but i have no resolve really, and it is not desperate
or angry or patient. it is a kind of hovering i do;
not angel-like, but stuck in time, the sempiternal,
wondering what you mean by this fuss in time.
i am waiting, but it is not the waiting of the dying,
not the waiting of the depressed or hopeless,
not the waiting of the lover.
i am waiting for you to cue that last crescendo;
i am waiting with cymbals poised or drumstick raised,
some dumb musician at the back,
waiting for your masterful hand
to drop; patient and eager, i'm poised
to make a sound that rallies everything
into a deafening rise, to focus the world's

grief and folly into finale. . . but there's no finale —
just applause and then ovation, and then
the galas and another symphony, another
show and it goes on — creation; while i wait,
poised for creation to get on with it.
and this christmas is just a longish pause. too long.
the time signature is wrong. in my heart, time flies
at the speed of love.

•

there are only two angels at the christmas
crib this year; i gave one to a child last summer;
i hope you do not miss him, jesus, or her or
whatever angels are; the two of them not lonely
for the third. i think they'll sing enough or
blow their horns or guide the wise men just as well, as two.
it's missing things, we are; you
fill in blanks, for angels or dry streets
that need festoons of white, for empty
holes unhappy people see in everything.
and you fill them with gifts sometime between
the eve and day; what you bring surprises us
every year; death mulching its incarnations,
lolling of children in the happy arms,
lovers complaining and making up with kisses — something for
everyone. what do you bring me this year? —
the heart-wrenched gifts of yesteryear;
eyes sorrowful for what i can't grasp,
wrinkles that grow furrows for your
sorrows, hopes for everyone else but me.
but you'll surprise me.
you'll bring me a lamborghini, or a
camera, no? i think not — i'm so bereft
i'll give nothing myself this year but love;
i'll come empty-handed at each neighbour's door
and shout glee and the plenitude of man on the planet,
enough for each other. . .

my heart's not fully in it, but you're working on it;
the miracle, a monster, me, and a third angel
to round off the tree.

●

angel of night
you come to me to tell me
everything is alright, to marry me
to days that aren't forgiven.
you come, out of the blue, out of dark, out of
the heart of jesus' middle, hurrying
past the leaves and snow and scurrying things;
you come in green and blue and violet — i no longer
have preferential colours or ideas about
how you should be;
because i am tired, and wounded and scarred with joys
and elated waste; because good things turned sour
and bad things were leaven;
because i hurried between the rough
doors of two things at once and they were one door,
wide open, past the signs of fear and stupidity
the world offered. i am here, lying down,
watching you come over me like
a summer cloud. the day before christmas.
i knew you would come. deep between the
canyons of my brain, mercy
erupts. and the pains and death and tribulation
no longer scatter me. i trail them like tin
cans tied to a cat's tail; because i know
my body is fodder, tinder, fuel, an ominous
ribboned package for some
presentment; for some christ-child with eyes
of galaxy blue and arms gentle as blades of grass
as i lie my face down to the planet, whispering,
listening, for the hurt and begotten, consoling
the tearful in myself and shushing away the ogres
from my eyes.
angel of night, you make the night go away.

you make day, a place to live.
bring whatever i have that pains
to the starmaker; tell him the rest is on the way,
a beaming smile, a certitude that puts to
rest my questions.

●

you are the angel i gave to a child.
you come back to me. though i thought i'd
lost you. it was not the angel of foreboding
and conclusions as i'd thought. it was not
the angel pointing earthward, or inward or
in any direction. you were the angel of love and pain,
or rather, simply the angel of the obvious
always escaping — that angels are made of the
little bit they pick up on earth and the
silken feathers of above. they are the marrying
point of pain and love, of sacrifice and wonder.
i know you now when i buy you in porcelain
or bronze, in brightening crystal and lead, or
marbled like my eyes, statued for christ.
i know you now and hope to see you in
all things without wings.
there are no wise men. you were the
days of their lives following the wounded
hope, the wizened and beleaguered — those who
followed their sorrow to the ends of the earth
for an answer and saw only themselves in
the night sky, mercy marrying the lust for god;
and the bandaged, ruined feet — coming to a manger
to find more of themselves, newly innocent
as the clockwork of the skies.
you do not fool me, angels; you see with my eyes
what i would see with grace — my self denuded
and radiant-hearted. the star of bethlehem
carried in kansas, peoria, illinois, and places
i don't care about, brought to His care.

Nights in the Country

In My Fifty-Third Year

i want snow to cover me. . .
to cast its arms around me.
to lavender me, to wash its ruby
lips upon me.

i want snow to forgive me:
its castles, its denizens, its brocade
arms; i am so lost without it

i love the snow, i will say to it.
all my childhood warblings
unmistakable in it.
be myself in it.

snow, come. want me.
God's mantle;
let them find a new face in it
when they discover me;

the mask of one not just me,
like me.

i am so much damage, beside the river,
beside the ice floes, without the liaison
of snow
what can i say or do?

once i was a cactus,
now i am the snow, wishing wishing.
be snow, be snow, be like snow
my young arms say, be world sheathed
on you, the screamer, the screaming world
muffled by the snow.

my white fluff stuff, my forgetfulness,
my reborn.
i cannot shovel, i cannot mourn.
i am for snow,
oh, i am for snow.

Wondering Me

i am the coyote man,
seeking non-representation.
just by name you know i'm he.

i have no gut, no inside.
just notoriety,
and you love me, sometimes.

you think my loneliness is
a condition, like yours, but more dramatic. . .

i am any number of metaphors,
among people who like metaphors.
i am the artery of our
knowing each other.

mercurial, if only i had been less
mercurial i would have been
something, somebody.

as it is, i stay awake all night
writing poems to coyotes, stars,
exporting goods to urban places.

i am having such a time.
i can take it. i can take it all.
rumour, expectation, regrets and
hope —
i am the narrative without myself, so many
narratives
seen, to be invisible;

see me, see me, says the lone voice of
the coyote. oh how can a coyote
want to be seen? watch me. watch me!
you have not been in the lone woods,
where a man wails.

Walking Sacred

will you forgive me, my friends,
for not being with you alive or dead,
all my lies, to get to you. i am not getting
to you.

betrayals of people, everyone betraying
jesus still, everyone betraying a dog,
a small animal, even me.

i forgive everything. i smile and smile.
i have seen it all.
you too, my friends, see it all.
forgive me.

there is nothing more fabulous than us.
they can hear us from neptune,
saturn, the lowing of forgiveness, the
galactic kind of mewl of being, one
human being against another,
absolving. there is such sweetness
there is poignancy in this or any
love note. forgive me. let us walk out
into the blue sky, the brown day.
kiss my cheeks. look, how i have

one arm too few to embrace you,
my denizens, you, my heart,
in need.

Sojourn

sometimes i am so gosh-darned
happy just to be writing poems not
for someone but because the sky says
yield what you got —

bones, mother and father stopping for
peaches beyond the skyway, chrome-polishing
those Chrysler fenders in Essex, those pools
we made love in at La Recondida.

the sky says yield, this, and the suitcases, chests
and trunks of love and tried love,
had love, half-requited to myself love.

i am half-stepping in my own urine
on the last day of my inevitable jaunt into God's
arms; i am picking sheaves of goldenrod and
greying wheat from the far hillsides like
a man in me i have sent away to harvest.

i am happy as a boy in Montreal, or anything,
not wanting to hear about going away.
i am happiest anywhere i am that God has brought me —
never an awful place.
i am happy to go nowhere, and yield and yield.
it is not prayer, exactly, or song,
and certainly not about leaving this world,
for i am in it like a paradise.

it is about the door opening and guests coming
in with flowers in their hair, each with a year
in the hand, or several and the yield, the sky
yields, like water refreshing the lowlands
and we just fill out the landscape of
talk and moons, nowhere but in our hearts,
so happily and in love with a planet
riveted to our feet.

For God, in Somnambulance

what a beautiful night,
balmy for november.
i half expected snow this time of year
and there you are, God, on the open
freeways between stars, twelve or thirteen
of them, between poplars and coyotes.

i come back thinking of you, from Mario's.
we've been discussing you again, him wanting me to read
that poem again about gobbling your grace over
dinner and revelling friends in '78; but he's more tired now,
building an empire; and me? well — toasted on funerals
and births; faithfully though, we think of you,
talk of you — tied in to that for years.
he's always got a new theory
on you, a turn of phrase, a theology that for
a corporate man astonishes. "fleshing God's
voice" was tonight's phrase; i'll work that in because he likes
being mentioned in my poems, like having a
friend at dinner.

his dad has Parkinson's, his mother aches from arthritis;
i touch her knees and wonder if there's any healing power
in my hands in spite of my stupidness.

he's lost a bit of hair, Mario has. i'm using a
cane some nights. we recall his holding court in
Yorkville, madman among yuppies, shouting poems
at the stars; well no you couldn't see stars there;
but we residued bricks with hominoid sweetness. how's that?
demanding a poem be recited, history overhauled with
metaphysic; he'd laugh and laugh, the funniest man alive —
like all my friends were, before money, Afghanistan,
Reagan, oh what the hell — before anything, we laughed —
before they unplugged the balloon of the world and let the air
out, who knows when — '68, last century, last year, who knows?

there's less romance. that's what the heart barometerizes. is that
a word? there's almost the word 'meteor' in that word.
that's what we are. i like that.
brief meteors, fizzling into aches and unimagination
around us.

there's a couple of things we're stumped by; not just the
zest of youth smudged by years; maybe at 50 all men
run out of things to say, except praying newly,
and so we're doing that, Mario and i. he goes to his mother's room
after board meetings, and prays.
maybe he does it to scare me, to show me empty
of heart. i think he makes too much money; but what's
eating him really, or us, is. . .

tonight we talk of crosses, how the world makes them;
how Jesus didn't have to die; that crosses are our language,
not God's;
he always makes it sound like it's our fault, Mario
does, but makes a hell of a good pasta and takes care
of 40 people. i take care of myself and am ready to blame God.

but tonight he has me almost convinced the cross i couldn't bear
at the monastery was a way of telling me to get out
so i did.
and i'm driving country roads, remembering.
i move my white collar across the table here; i've just
taken it off to write you a love letter, like it was in the way,
like it was choking me, like i want to find you nakedly.

i smoke, and write long poems and look up at a few stars,
and remember your visits, as if you were some cousin who'd
stayed for awhile.
i'm glad you're gone, the idea of you, at least. now
i can be alone with my real God, the nameless, unnaming
one who says as little as how i live, in a shack in
country woods.
i wish Mario this peace, as he falls asleep tonight.

and his God with him.
for we are only together when we pray, my friends and i.
may this poem be a prayer; no! a preamble to his
tucking us in.
take care of your own, tonight, my God, your children,
all of whom i love; all of us in the same dream together,
where our souls walk out of us and meet in the
plaza or in fields, away from dialogue and orbit,
adrift in each other like poppies in the wind,
swaying in different directions but humming our
little heads off — love, love, with a little baton
of wind orchestrating us — love, love, asleep —
never waking apart from each other.

Father on the Shore

when I see you standing on
the seashore, on those rocks, looking out
over the blue mediterranean, i see myself
standing on shoals on lake ontario;
i had not known we had this
connection until i find your picture
in mother's grab bag of things; you in 1940;
as usual, in a neat suit, with a winning
smile for the sun and water; if i'd known
i'd come to love what you loved,
from bolex cameras to mancini music, to shoals. . .
what else is left, the way we die? if i'd known
we'd waste time the same way, parked
under bridges, musing at air and light.
had i known we'd take our time
in the same way. . . how absurd.
i didn't have two words for you when i was fourteen.
i thought you slow-minded, as i am now. but i see you were
pausing between loved things, your
rituals of cleaning tools, just so,
just so, the way i do the dishes first and
light a cigarette before a poem — the pace, our blood
together; i would pour that blood back into
your bones if i could.

father, i see your feet on those rocks. they're my feet; i see
your knuckles — they're mine. i remember your
bristly cheek on mine, and trying to wrestle you
to the ground. but what i want to say is. . . take me
with you; no. . . let us see the same wave together as i write this:
one step from a churn of water frozen in time.
and there's your smile; the same one's in my head, but forced.
not quite your smile —
that perfect smile i took for foolishness.

we raced once on the annapolis shore.
it's on film. mother must have taken it.
you raced ahead, in a neat suit;
you couldn't resist it — you won
the race. in the film you run towards the camera and the last
frame captures your eyes, and me lagging behind on
clumsy teenage legs.
teach me quickness of heart.
come to my heart that is beginning to understand.
i thought you were falling behind, in thought and years,
but you understood everything at the speed of light, so slow
as to enjoy that world that i can't spin into a halo however
fast i go; catch up to me father;
rather, hold your hand back on
that last frame — hold it fast behind you.
reach out with your joy,
for your slow and only son.

For My Dead Mother

i'm phoning you now because my
life is mad. did you know that?
i said nothing to you for years,
and you would have assured me i wasn't
mad, typically, like a mother; you are
buried half a mile away, God has me
by the teeth and i am writing poems
between the pains he gives me in my fingers
and my brain. He says you were too serious
about Him, and thanks you for teaching me
to take Him seriously. you know that.

but i would have taken Him seriously —
the beautiful, at some point. still,
you taught me beauty; He, the hunger.

but i phone you today to see if you
are still singing as you did at 35 in that
lyric voice of yours. i used to wonder who
you were singing for when i was five —
the curtains as you cleaned them, the stove,
the sunlight — i caught on to the
sunlight coaxing you. i sing for just
about anything too, you know.

you used to say i got the poet in me from
you, though you never understood a blessed
word; you heard i was a poet and you knew,
your singing and my watching you;
it brought your yen for God into the open.
that's poetry.

my life is mad, though. you wouldn't
recognize it. i am in the darndest places,
maybe 'cause i have no child to
watch me sing, i sing in barns, under bridges,

in bars, in places you would not understand,
singing not for you exactly, but finding
God in the song, the notes so desperate,
making Him up as i go along.
maybe you did too, but cheerfully.
i'm not cheerful,
being conceived during the war and all, or
maybe the twentieth century just got
my goat, maybe i redeem badly, like a gene
that wanted to make its mother's insides
happy, 'cause you'd lost a son by the time
you had me; so maybe singing was flying
above hurt for you. maybe i feel that hurt,
or you just left me with it, but adding, "you're not mad".
you left me something you forgot to take with you.
and so i phone. can you be shocked anymore?
i am your poet with a vengeance for God,
but without your sweet resignation, your
occasional sweet resignation. not often enough
i stop my warbling and just smile —
my life is mad you know; without your
song, the ending notes, you did not teach me.

The Child

i thought I heard a child
shouting for help;
in the dusk coyote twilight,
in an autumn, subdued;

i thought he might have been
stuck in a well, in a hole in a
barn, but it was the voice of
me, or something like me.
why does God send some ambiguity?
to see if you'll get up from your chair and
go outside and listen which i did, being cautious
for the world, is it exercise to see
if your conscience is still going?

i'll look for the child in me then. is
he stuck in my craw, in a dream, is it he who i
drive miles to like a crazy rabbit in the
dark, accomplishing this and that,
to drag him from a well? can i help him?
is he in front of me right now, shouting?
am i deaf to my yearning song?

what do you need, little one? i watch my hands, my arms,
a shiver runs for almost touching you.
you are there after all. i feel it.
there was no going outside,
my mother's son. have i forgotten you
behind the books and bank towers and melodies
of love?

the barns grow dark, i hear no child. far away
crickets mull away what's left of autumn.
i am left with "help" inside me, in the deafening
silence that will not take me home.

oh God, now You give me a blue-dark cloud
in the evening, to fold open like sheets
and find myself sleeping, like
what i would cradle in my arms; myself.

i hear a child, every day, and sometimes
the volume is raised, saying days are short.
You safekeep him, my orphaned self, until
my eyes get better and the dark won't keep me from him.

Burials

who did you bury?
you buried everybody
waiting for the bogeyman to come
time running out —
you'd better make the most of
dragonflies and things

Rocco is showing me his garden
like so many others
why don't they grow accordions
always fig trees and fig trees
why don't they grow forgiveness?

I am the burial man.
I pray over coffins of plutonium
alabaster right through the coffin
ignoring the stench of flowers
which I cannot bear.

I buried Carmen, others,
and I grow them in my poems.
I buried my mother
and I live in the woods.

there is no
haunting.

so many
waiting for
love letters.

Song

What is there to be afraid of?
I have seen the dead,
                    their small
messages like puppies
beside them. Go away, they said.
So much love, used up. One woman
said her husband passed into her
like breath.
    She prayed for that feeling to come
again
and again.

Harvesters, take no heed of the
      spelling of things.

The Hands of Widows

the hands of widows
row upon row.
like a locket, a keepsake,
i give them my hand.
i have walked in mausoleums
kept men from climbing in with
the dead.
there is no door to death. it is
always taking place in someone else's
clothes.

the dead take my clothes,
whatever is handy.
they love me.
and recommend me.

New Prayer

today we get ready to go away.
what for. . . for the chance that
the townships might have leaves on
them still; we need some leaves,

today, if there's time we go to
the lake; water baptizes, refreshes.

we'll phone tony because he is man enough
to say i miss you on the phone.

today we'll try to forget and forgive
the past again, and refurbish the
smiles we smiled at
for years, even though they betrayed
you since, and you couldn't forgive.
but you couldn't forget
those smiles like cut-outs in your heart.
nothing to fill them with but God and
diversion.

today we get ready to go to the townships
and drive, the four of us, hoping we won't
destroy it;
when you're a kid you don't think of
such things;
you don't think of harold drunk with too much
money, or sally so buried in hurts she
gets hysterical three husbands later.

when you're a kid you go out to the street
and those spanking new faces, tough or nice,
are a million to choose from; if you don't
find happiness under this rock or that, or behind that bush
or on this cricket-filled night, the dice will come
up different on another day. . .

today i am almost convinced i go through motions,
i gear up hope, an enthusiastic little man in me
won't quite go to sleep. . .

today, world, be nice; don't let me paint you
with the bad colours; be stronger than my
disappointment. God's grace, outdo yourself, for
all of us. don't let us tag you with ulterior motives
for the kiss someone smacks on us.

let's find leaves and prayers that say we consecrate
this moment past our burning of what will hurt
to remember.

as simple as that water dripping from the faucet —
our silver wants just dropping
into each other, filling, filling, and the sun through
each of them, shimmering — God, straightforward,
with no lesson about learning to forgive and or how to love.

we love, oh let us.

A Little Verse for my Sister and I

i think she was schizophrenic.
she left me in the springtime of
my life.
we gave her blood to drink, my sister and i.

my sister and i were always giving blood in
those days. my sister of the left
star and the moon with flowers;

anyway she drank and drank at God's well
around which my sister and i had planted
flowers.
so many came and went in that garden,
it's enough to make you want to believe in
saints.

i dreamt i ran into don knotts and he said
what a good guy andy griffith was — how the
show gave hope to a lot of people.
andy was a cadaver among others in the dream.
laid out, white, but without a shroud. . .

i remember whistling the theme with
him and opie going fishing; everyone wanted
to go fishing but we gave blood my sister and i.
we were a little less pedantic in tuscany;

it looks like autumn outside my window, but
it is january and I have no ways to tell
people how some have left me.
i will go to the bank and put in amounts
of money in a country where people are thirsty and not
poor.

it was many years ago. i was in love with this
schizophrenic; i only say that about her because
she came and went. never kept still. the world
is like that, or was. now it is
just traumatized,
unable to go fishing, and i live
in a cabin in the woods; well not really in the
woods, but on the moon, the crepuscular
willowy side; my sister has learned
to paint flowers.

we hurt, as many do, in the vessels of blue humanity
given to us by the well-maker.
the blood-giving has given beautiful sunsets and
rivers of gold and jasmine sky.

my sister was right about that much, suffering
made a bouquet of an uncomprehending, dumb
and milk-papping world.

she does not believe in God — my sister. i do.
but she believes in his many arms and hairs,
and flow of syllables, gentle and hard as "kill" and
"born". so we look back on a schizophrenic world,
and remember giving and wish good things
to one who left me, us, or anyone who left themselves
for awhile; God's well, empty and waiting,
in a garden that is by now our hearts.

There Was This Fellow

i look forward to nothing.
today is about a day i have lost a dream.
yet another;
and don't quite have the reach to
get another

or maybe don't want to; for i have
tasted enough of each that i can piece together
the whole lot, the giant plan of love i am
destiny for.

today i think i would have cried at the loss
of this one when i was younger. now i smile.
is it easy to smile when the last part of a dream
is still unseen?
maybe i will weep again when i am within reach of
something wonderful. today is the fabric
of stitched things. i say thank you,
and the angels that bring some understanding
of the in-between, i say thank you to,
and ask for guidance from,
to understand, even though the understanding
will take passion from my mouth — but i
don't think so. i think i am passionate
in a new way, the screaming and rhapsodic behind all
blessed things.
i have been brought here and it is good,
with my heart in my mouth, the
guy in me getting around to living
in spite of himself, like a wall he walked into
that he didn't know was there, thinking he knew
his way around the whole house.

a flower appears and stuns him, or the walk didn't need
to be forced, or he's shedding the cocoon of himself—
butterfly, passion, wings, whatever.

Sky, be like me, and for me, on this day,
when i am almost sorry.

Christ

the heart has turned to water;
— water, where the heart has split
like a river carving the stone, the
river of pain turned
to mercy, turned
to healing,
water in place of heart;

a roar unlike niagara, the euphrates,
a river like a blind eye shedding rivers of
water.

thirst —
to wake up, mouth parched
like a desert, dreaming thirst for what was,
what might have been; when the water

is for healing, not drinking;

the waters of love and pity,
are the slaked dreams of the father.

dreams come true. the splintered
ones are His business.
like a snake eating its tail,
there is only healing and healing.

what was wanted in the first place,
beyond reach, forever.

to go home, to
pluck the apple
of desire — a name, a place,
an unfulfilled.

one death, and the healing is done.

and
this thirst
flowing through the cracks of my heart
for everyone.

Among the Byways of Above

do you want a man who looks
like me?
appalled at man, appalled at moon,
under the orange bloody,
necessary moon, appalled at love,
at a man like me.

nowhere. scouring. so happy to have his
face in the stars, buried in the stars, tail
wagging like exonerated hell.
a man like me so lost in the semblance
of, so lost, such oh such a carnivore
along the leaves and plants of people.
seeing blood, seeing carnage,
and still lifting a child to the air,
such an appalling idiot of himself —
love, two-sided, imbecilic with the sun,
and all the wishes.

Where I Live

A bungalow in the field.
Busloads of remembered things.
The summer sky.
   Rolling hills.

   Coyotes.
    Mass at 5.
   Burials,

a dirt road.

   Sunflowers.
Cactus ornaments.

Fifties things.
        Love in corners.

                    ●

I melt
in Him who loves stars and things.

                    ●

Between the stalks of corn
I forget how to spell.
The sun and its tray of jewels
      repeats that
the moon is a chrome-faced lover.
        The moon drags the clouds
. . . sometimes you want
to give
as God in his munificence sends flies.

Nights in the Country

coyotes in the field, beautiful
    shredders two or three
cheek to jowl.
        the dogs hate them, bark against
howl, an orange moon, a train whistle,
hotshot stars, myself, a face in the
windowpane, God, electrons up and down
my fingers   enumerating death
     abyss.   i am full of the talk
of my friend gabe an hour ago.
i am full of the talk of
       coyotes beautiful scavenging
dog-hungry,
incoherent brothers.
bless them.

Alone

there is the fear of the dark
returning, the rooms closing in,
the bottom of a well,
there is what can only be alleviated by
distraction,
like a plank at sea, like birds flying back after
an ancient winter, like mother or father
come to get you.

there is the exhaustion of weeping.
and duty, footsteps, movement — strong
sonata of movement carrying the ornery,
guts, heart, appendages.
there is such beauty in the leaves and trees.
heard — tell — of beauty in the brooks and stones,
heard beauty in the stars and the various;
this anger aimed at God and messengers is
beautiful too, like a warrior with hair on fire.

there is the event of mosquito and osprey,
of light switches and absurd history;
any and all event, for all the good anything
will do when they come and collect me,
little man
with the rage of a sunset in him,
ordinary man with a planet to spoon from.

The Simple Breeze in the Willow

A Little Song of Want

I have been through here before.
It is a familiar valley with portraits
of familiar loss on the rock walls.
The customary yodelling of warning
and bequest.
It ain't Atlantis and it ain't Innisfree.
This is a journey where all you loved
betray you.
You simply get a haircut and have done with it.
Bitterness will only bog you down.
It is nonchalance you want; that is, simply to
walk in your own blood and not be nauseated.

Here now, are the daffodil and faun, within
reach of your distances, yearning to be seen for
what they are, like you.
Through the bramble of apparent need you go,
through the arbour of refreshing gaiety;
the lions of discomfort and disease gnarl their angry
snouts in your direction. . .
past the sirens and ameliorations,
past your brother, the kite, hear the song of the
little one in you, the one not fed, so long not fed,
and promise him the one he would grow into,
yourself. Tell him a story,
the lonesome narrative of your life, and fall asleep
with him, and wake up one,
married to the morning and the blossoms, so shy,
and forthcoming.

When Joe Cries

when joe cries, baby moons fall
down, hundreds of songs by jane morgan and
monica lewis go for ice-cream — his daughters become
chatelaines and stars,
his dreams come true, love rides a grand stallion
into the gettysburg fields, his mother loves him
and my friend becomes himself
as god nods, that great outstanding nod
gives us that picnic, that ordination, that carousel ride
we had jumped on the orbiting planet for —
so much ado, so much ado,
finally the moment happening, this life starting
minus the aches and pains, the damned planet
between our toes like bad grass.
and we are kings, with fires in our hair, of passion
and fireflies like weak nostalgia, like a halo,
hardly wanted. . . and the laughter, naked,
like a white star, at the incipience of, beginning of,
this freshborn infant of.

House and Garden

I do not know You, You are not there.
You perfect me through pain,
but I want something other than You.
I want to rest.

I am tired of looking at myself in the
picture with me riding through
the Arches National Park, looking for a star
in my left hand.
I am tired of listening to Glenn Miller with
the dead wife I never had,
of dreaming the dreams of others, of riding
the sleeves of their dreams like butterflies,
foreign and sad. I want to walk with You through
the arbour and be happy.
Today, I want to be loved, unequivocally and
known for the sentiments I had for everyone,
the living, the dead, the imagined.
And I imagined so much, for You to have something to
build; like land for Your working, my heart was.
If I am a soul, take it away or let me be as gentle with it
as I am with the moth at my doorstep. I take it in and
give it a home because it wants light. I am not much
different, Lord; may I be taken in only
by angels, and of the good variety.
Let my faith be steel that brandishes nothing
but the wings I feel inside of me,
so tender and reaching for sunlight,
like the day I was born without regret.
Like that, take me in; and close the door on
no one.

Cowboy on Horse in Desert

Little cowboy, painted on
a paint-by-numbers picture
found in a junk shop. I have had you for ten years
now. I carry you with me wherever I go
because you are so lonely and never quite make
it through to the canyon arches you're aimed at.
Someone aimed you at something, forever.
Kinda like me and a couple of dreams.
I wish I could paint in
an arrival for you.
As it is, we keep each other company you and I.
Your icons become my icons, that cactus presiding over your
path, the cotton candy clouds in blue I see some days,
the arid dirt and boulders, that rock face that
looks like the snout of a benevolent large dog, neither
asleep nor threatening, like the poised
chances of my own life.

There are so many wonderful paintings,
cowboy, but you and I, we are simpler than that.
We are done with shades, and textures and the meaning of
tilted faces in amber light —
we are doggedly going, you and I, called by neither oasis
nor homestead, just moving in the brash sun
that neither parches nor woos.

What I watch is your stillness, caught in neither leaving nor
arrival — an image of me. I could almost take you
out and feed you, put you to bed, tell you stories
of the prairie, my prairie,
and I wonder if whoever made you, loved you as much as
I do. . . an old man, given to the soil, before he could give you
away? — a dreamy housewife, pining for the springs
that her husband hadn't? I don't think it was a little
girl who made you — you are too full of
unremitted hope for a child to know much about.

Perhaps you are just a factory thing,
the lineaments of stasis just right for the
frozen moment as I dream it.

Still, it gave you birth, little cowboy.
I even made a journey to Saguaro, after staring
at your cactus for a year. Another year, perhaps I'll become you.
We want to represent our heart to others, don't we?
Isn't that all we want to be for each other,
identifiable pictures of what we give and can't give?

Your sagebrush is badly done, your shadows
cheat, the peaked stone towers in the arroyo
unmatched from anything out here. . .
so much like me, your world,

and the flowers, the total absence of flowers,
and you seem at peace with that, as if
you sang them in your heart
like a ditty you might be humming under the
brim of your hat.

You are satisfied. I can see that,
and you are better than any Moses, or extravagaria.
You are my little self, what little there was, taken
into a future that never comes.
Whether I have my glasses on or not,
I can see you clearly,
unlike what I have made of myself,
where you have found a home.

I can wish you nothing you do not
already have,
and that is your wish for me.

Sogni d'Oro

That which was alive
is beyond resuscitation
like a blindness, beyond which
the world is unrecoverable, just
happy remembrances scuttling like
ghosts.
It doesn't matter after awhile
in life, who killed what;
it is the impoverished you have to live with,
the soiled,
it is the weary voice of hope
like a baying thing in the woods — you
want to feed it and bring it food but as much
as anything else, you want to kill it, put it
out of its misery, to let the carnations and brambleweed
do their thing, irrespective of your drama.
You'd like to see life carry on without you,
as a gift and a kind of retribution for your
unloved miracles.
There is not much in the broken barn

and in another weathered day,
but beauty in inescapable forms
for the young ones and the rosary of pain
in the hands of the old.
Dutifully, you map the stars in as simple
a thing as a poem, the fabric of your skin
and trust that catches constellations
and dead music;
the many ways of saying things have been
tossed to the side of the road in that erratic
drive to your presumed salvation —
and you are left with a weed by the highway,
and a fortunate sun reaching through branches, arranging
its leaves in a conjecture or two.
It doesn't matter who killed what.

Messages of reprieve and suspended hate
are in your heart; you might almost waft them
to the perpetrators like a kiss across
the mountains of horrendous promise
and disillusion,

like a boat you might all fit into, like children,
hugging and clapping at the moon,
oh so alone and sufficient in happinesss, without
mother, unhearing of grief,
and so dumb to tragedy.
That is my final wish to my fellow murderers,
whose dreams are closeted in the
same heart as mine.

The Wild Wild West

This house loves me.
I always said so.
The chipmunks and squirrels have absented
themselves for the summer, as if they had gone
on a trip. I assume they'll be back in the spring
when they forage for food.
I'd better leave some things for them
where they can find them.

Perhaps the cat will leave a kitten in return for
a bowl of milk. I haven't seen
the garter snake for awhile;
funny how they disappear and know how not to be seen
like in any desert.
No need for a palm or cactus. Animals know the desert.
It takes us forever to realize it,
to live in it, to admit we are tired and thirsty.
You wake up one morning and you admit you're a
desert dweller. It's no good telling the young
or the obtuse that the skyscrapers are
delusional, or that the highway looks more and
more like death valley, or that the last
real visitors were lost and looking for their lives.

I used to travel, but landscapes are of the heart,
lush or barren, we make them out to be what we are.
This might be handy when you are without house
and without window, happy at last to be in anything,
ready to start again with God's own eyes,
impartial to want and lakeside;
to be wise at last in the eyes
and to see what is under your nose —
the present, like a given flower.

More than that. . . such that this house glows.
It is more than what might be given, to a man
learning to walk.
The sunlight and pines are a bonanza, as far as I'm concerned —
so many metaphors to live in at last,
and so little to explain to what heeds, or needs to know.
It is I who need to know my habitat,
this blind heart and foolish will.
I must treat myself as gently as I would the
animals for I'm a good deal more naive
and unwitting of my predator soul.
So that my house includes my supplication
and humility. I lean against it and only lean
slightly,
like a question leading to a river or a town,
as if I had some respect at last for what brings me here,
ignorance and a good deal of grace.

Admonition to Our Lonely Selves

It is the sadness of the incomplete that kills me —
the cadavers walking around with bouquets
in their arms, shouting remembrance, of the near
solstice days, of loss and harmonies forgotten.
It is this mixture of grief and hope, destroys;
the priest who says he wanted to be a fairy godmother,
the woman who falls in love at the wrong moment of
her life, the 95-year-old woman who scared herself
in the bathroom one day by remembering how old
she was.

I am sick of the incomplete and the completedness
that was never in the scheme of things,
the friendship that became itself, after all the forcing,
the poems that got written, in spite of joy,
the vision that we are of ourselves, after
the dead illusions;

it is as if we were stupid and brought all the
Cinderellas to the ball, while we stayed home.

I am happy, it appears, today, with dessicated apples
under the tree and chipmunks, named,

and a ladder that goes nowhere because it is made of one
split log and narrowed at one end; it is made for apple picking —
you climb up half way, and. . . no more ladder — it props
itself against the branches nicely; you pick, and there is
nowhere further to climb — it points at the stars,
where you are perched to reach for apples.
There's no use dreaming of stars; they are for seeing,
but the garden is all yours.

How happy I would have been to meet my limitations
when I was young. I would have gathered them like good
dogs and kept warm by them; we would have been friends
and they would have guarded me from such aspirations
as gnawed the silken thread of every hope.
Even now I look at a dowager sky on the horizon and dream
silver and childish blue — I am never still
with my completions and incompletions.

Whoever you are, walking into my life, take note of this,
and the same sad malady that winds about your head — may we never
finish what we have started in each other.
Let dawn find her children,
who did not know where they were,
happy and unafraid of the dark.

Love's Threnody

I don't know much about loving.
it comes when it will.
the gifts pull back, the horseshoe comes when it
will — the shower of stars has its call, the
shooting stars must be seen so quickly;

I always leave the door open now —
I have no illusions about looking down the
road to see what's coming: pilgrim, or wayfarer,
horror, or blessing.
I am not even fooled by the heart taking note of things,
a song, an angel hair, or a sweet narrative
of personal destiny.

I could say so many things —
I had the questions all planned out — they had
such dutiful and sugary answers;
I am surprised to find the questions still in your
mouth or in the human creature so poised and fatigued.
Funny how they think the answers forthcoming,
my compatriots in grief and oasis —
I am so little fooled. I stare at rocks and pebbles,
the dull glint of a palm as it drops its shadow on the
desert floor while they drink and drink inexhaustably,
my lovers of life — nattering with rattled tongues
and fluttering hearts of the prize just over
the hill, the few miles before God gathers all His forces
and makes the trip worthwhile;
I know so little about loving.
I love us travelling together and dread the next
great call to this destination and that —
the hope that dresses as a waylay, the map buried
for so long, that clue to the happiness right under one's nose.
I resent this fuss about what's coming to us,
or we to it.

I love you any old way in syllables and concurrences,
in dogged agreements about where you should go
and what I should do — I will say anything
to make the human stop and linger until the
end of time, until we face each other, the moment like
a simple desert breeze between us.

Poem

Funny how we never have the time
we thought. We keep thinking the dramas
will go on; when will Vanessa find her Prince Charming?
— though she has settled for a boring man from Timmins —
when will the wolves leave the sheepfold and let
the lambs come in again, when will the beauteous arrive,
prepared by how many books and warm-up performances?
And so the heart of a sixteen-year-old still beats
in us. We still think
the drama has yet to unfold,
when it has; Vanessa is married thirty years now,
the wolves have taken up residence, the gala
performance never did arrive, or did, in
a hand-hold under moonlight, so quiet it was missed.
What was needed was a director with
a sense of time and rehearsal schedules.
It wasn't until we saw the wrinkles on our palms
that we twigged on to something,
but we figured the car would make it to Cincinnatti,
Minneapolis, without a tune-up, before the coast
and its palms and soft-sea breezes.

Then the cast starts dying, the loveable
faces, the mean ones, endings get written, the plot
revised and you are left with a sense of
divine will or cheap prognostication.
You knew things might come to this, and that, you
might have guessed it, is one version of the plot;
as if you had been sitting out of the picture, quite alone,
requesting uselessly, another take.

Meaning

Today I am wrestling with death
but it is not death really
but sameness,
denied happiness.
A transparent world
yells its vanity, women
on the radio, men on the
highways,
my forsaken appearance
in your life.

It has tailed me like a dog,
this uselessness.
I hate having words for it,
this peripheral skating around
what bugs us.
Nothing matters and the hues of love
appease for awhile
but it is not love we want
or it would have stilled us
long ago.

What bothers us is being godlike for an hour
and falling into frailty —
that need to go through the
mountain pass again
with flowers bunched in our hands
like laurels above the stinging snow,
knowing this time, we will not die,
— that the heroism will succeed.

We want do it again, this time without fear —
the child, the marriage, the tentative
walk in the isolate moonlight;
we will do everything again,

and this time we will do it with faith.

The Calm Before the Rain

Today is the day
I see through the designs
of my own foolish will and the
the improbable will of others
and understand God offering His hand
in a flower. Today, a red-letter day,
I keep still; all desires have come to the stream.
The mild thundering outside is like myself plowing
through thick skies to arrive at some
heeding and finding only soft rain
washing my silted efforts.

Today disappointment has found me out
in the love I had not expected and the love
I had thought myself capable of;
today I see there are no events of love,
only the giving and getting of it,
and the only crime, the willful cessation of song.

Today, I am going away to
where the landscape and myth unfold their
arms to me.

The stories of love I take with me
are safekept and of no interest to anyone
but the badger and the ongoing seasons
that drape their memorabilia like tinsel on
lakefront and escarpment.

To leave the world is never a pretty thing,
unless a child has vacated the premises,
until you see the darkness as inevitable,
until you exhaust your useless hopes
and become the body of God's will.

The maddening merry-go-round and your eyes
are of no avail. The phone rings and you are never there.
The sky darkens. The animals have taken shelter for awhile.
It is time for a meditation.
Like a thing in the womb; it is the hour of dumb wisdom —
the moment you are closest to God,
before the awful fall
to senses and heartfelt things.
Let the rain come to wash my entry to this world,
this same and new place.
Let stillness be a lesson I bring with me
as I make much of the thrush piping its way
through the dark.

The North Moon and the Priest

Faced with the loss of
something, when
change takes from me again
the haven, the embodiment of leaves
and galaxy,

when the roads open up their
mouths to delude again,

when the darkness smothers the lamp,
and the weasels of chance gnaw with their
mean souls,

I have a certain heart,
and a destiny
to find under the rocks, the willow's descent — the
tiresome clambering of stars to achieve ovation —

I am there
with a stomach for grief,
and the shell game that God metes out.

I am aubade, the sanctuary of justification
by which the child can hope,
the widow sing, the fisherman make himself
to be a lover of stars.

My certain heart is all you have of me
when you have done with the deliveries
of time, and the pups, the unfed sagas,
and the possibility you took or not —

find me, waiting,
for all the joy uncovered, covering you
in what joy I have.

Oh Resilient Heart

Resilient heart,
sequestered and so new,
so happy to see the mountains and
the sunrise, you have come so
nicely out of shadows
and into the blue,
having heard there was much to be had,
through no doing of our own.

You astonish me; when I had
weighted you with some metaphors,
you claimed your own.
I had not found you as I thought I had,
so I could not have killed you.
You are not water after all, or crevasses,
or canyons; you are what has been
spared of me,
like a bird flown over the distant
ranges.

Resilient, lithe thing of the air,
you make me laugh,
care-free of my opinion, you enjoy the
skies and invent clouds and imagine nothing.

You are certain of us,
like the day that will come, no matter what.

There is no music to follow you,
resilient heart, no need of faces and
caresses; let me offer you something, anything. . . like one hand
in another, like names or kisses;
let me give you the doors and scented evenings by
which you escaped.

But you defy me with
your sufficient song.
Beyond anything gathered,
you surprise me with the
sunlight of a grace
when I again mistake the day
on garden walls for moonlight.

Imbiancato

A note of thanks to you when
all is said and done, for the little cowboy,
for the sonata, for the now and again
shimmer of sun that reinstitutes, reinvests.
A note for the surprises I ask you to safeguard from me
lest I marry them to my grief.
Take care of me in my blindness.
Teach me to say a prayer when I am out of words.
Remind me that hope outlives the flesh.

Give me that happiness I said would straighten me out.
And if I have already had it, forgive me.
I offer you these moments here in front of me
where I am less beleaguered than I was —
moments you gave to me. I am through being fed up
with returning your gifts. I give you back everything
you gave with the incarnate music you wanted
wrapped around it.
What you want with such music is beyond me,
the lace of tears, the jewelled warbling,
the hurts hosannaed on a moonlit
night of stars,
the scream at death, beaten into faith so simple
it wound around a girl's head like a ribbon.

I admit finally, my footsteps are not my own.
I surrender, as I did to all great things, to the plausible
fabrication of your hand.
I dream of little cowboys, many of them,
all happy to find a campfire at night with the increased
consolation of your voice in wind and whippoorwill.

I will walk today into the empty sojourn
of my life and look forward to the nearest stream
and that nocturnal conversation between us

where I offer you my tears
and you will raise them like a river between
stars and stars.
There's not much more this heart would
care to divine.
This note of thanks I place somewhere at your feet,
a man on the planet.

PIER GIORGIO DI CICCO was born in Arezzo, Italy, and raised in Baltimore, Montreal and Toronto. He lives in the countryside north of Toronto.